The FACT ATTACK series

Awesome Aliens
Beastly Bodies
Cool Cars
Crazy Creatures
Crucial Cricket
Dastardly Deeds
Deadly Deep
Devastating Dinosaurs
Dreadful Disasters
Fantastic Football
Gruesome Ghosts
Incredible Inventions
Mad Medicine
Magnificent Monarchs
Nutty Numbers
Remarkable Rescues
Rowdy Rugby
Spectacular Space
Super Spies
Vile Vampires

FACT ATTACK

ROWDY RUGBY

IAN LOCKE

MACMILLAN CHILDREN'S BOOKS

First published 1999 by Macmillan Children's Books

This edition published 2012 by Macmillan Children's Books
a division of Macmillan Publishers Limited
20 New Wharf Road, London N1 9RR
Basingstoke and Oxford
Associated companies throughout the world
www.panmacmillan.com

ISBN 978-1-4472-2445-7

1 3 5 7 9 8 6 4 2

A CIP catalogue record for this book is available from
the British Library.

Printed and bound by CPI Group (UK) Ltd, Croydon CR0 4YY

DID YOU KNOW THAT . . .

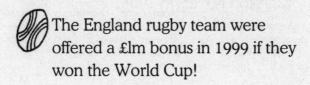

Rugby League began in 1922 when the Northern Rugby Football Union was formed at the George Hotel in Huddersfield – 20 clubs voted to resign from the Rugby Union Association.

The England rugby team were offered a £1m bonus in 1999 if they won the World Cup!

One of the most unusual players in world rugby history is Lewis Capes. 1.93 metres tall (six foot four) and 130 kg, he gave up American football to play for Leicester Tigers in England in 1997. He has since retired from rugby as well.

1

Rugby injuries are so common they rarely make the front page. But one injury did hit the headlines in April 1999 – Prince William had to have an operation after he fractured his hand playing rugby.

George Henry 'Titer' West scored a record 53 points (10 goals and 11 tries) in a Rugby League match, playing for Hull Kingston Rovers in 1905.

Irish Rugby Union player Nigel Carr had to quit the game after he was injured. In 1987 he was hit by the blast of an IRA bomb which killed Lord Justice Gibson and his wife.

Western Samoa staged its first rugby international, against Fiji, at Apia in 1924. So that people could get to work, the game began at seven in the morning! There was something not quite right about the pitch – on the halfway line there was a large tree!

The New Zealand national Rugby Union side are known as the 'All Blacks'. The 'All Whites' are Swansea rugby players. (And the New Zealand Rugby League team are called the 'All Golds'.)

The name 'All Blacks' for the New Zealand rugby side was given to them by the *Daily Mail* newspaper on 12 October 1905 in honour of their victory the day before, when they had beaten Hartlepool clubs 63–0.

The largest ever rugby crowd gathered to watch Australia versus New Zealand at Stadium Australia for the Bledisloe Cup in 2001.

Jonny Wilkinson became the leading points scorer in English rugby with 1,179 points recorded.

Thomas Gisborne Gordon was probably the most unusual international ever. He had only one hand! His right hand was lost after a shooting accident when he was a child. He played on the wing for Ireland three times in 1877 and 1878. Ireland lost every match.

One of the great stars of world rugby was New Zealander Jonah Lomu. He claimed he was born to play rugby. Lomu's statistics are pretty impressive. His neck was 60 cm, his arms were 94 cm each, his chest was 135 cm and his hips were 125 cm! He has now retired.

On 27 December 1982, Peter Richmond, a policeman, was referee for the match between Abingdon and Didcot. Following a punch-up, the match became a free-for-all. The two captains were called over by the referee. He said, 'I've had enough, I'm fed up with it.' All thirty players were then sent off!

The Saracens rugby club launched a degree in rugby at Buckinghamshire Chilterns University in 1999!

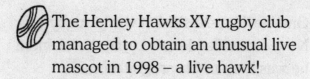The Henley Hawks XV rugby club managed to obtain an unusual live mascot in 1998 – a live hawk!

The scores 4 and 7 were not possible in Rugby Union until 1971 when the scoring was changed. A score of 5 is now no longer possible.

Gavin Hastings of Scotland scored 44 points in the match against the Ivory Coast in the World Cup of 1995.

There are six ways of scoring in rugby:
1.   A try.
2.   A goal.
3.   A penalty goal.
4.   A dropped goal.
5.   A goal from a mark.
6.   A penalty try.

Willie John McBride, who played in five British Lions tours and played for Ireland 63 times, said after his first game of rugby that he would 'never play that ruffians' game again'!

 In 1998 the All Blacks claimed that their team, who were beaten by South Africa in the World Cup final in 1995, were poisoned the night before the match.

 Every South African side visiting Britain brings with them a mounted 'Springbok Head' which they award to the first team to beat them or the team which gives them the hardest match.

Henry Cooper, who became famous as a champion British boxer in the 1960s, objected to playing Rugby Union while doing his National Service in the British army.

Jonah Lomu, the legendary All Blacks star, returned to rugby in 1997 after a serious illness. A year later he was offered a part in the new Bond film *The World is Not Enough*.

 Up to two substitutes were allowed in rugby from March 1968. The first sub was F. P. Bresninan of Ireland in the British Isles team vs. Western Transvaal, South Africa, on 18 May 1968.

 Barry John and Willie John McBride, the Welsh and Irish rugby stars, have both appeared on *This is Your Life*.

 The roughest Rugby Union match up to 1939 was said to be the Wales against Ireland match at Belfast in 1914. The Wales side was captained by a man of God, the Reverend J. Alban Davies! The Wales pack was so ferocious it was known as the 'Terrible Eight'.

Australia have a phenomenal record when it comes to the Rugby League World Cup – they won it for 24 years in a row, before losing to New Zealand in 2008!

Tommy Holmes, a scrap merchant in the north of England, was known to accept any deal. His oddest purchase was a sick lion from a circus. Though he looked after the lion, the sickly creature soon died. Tommy arranged for the remains of the lion to be dealt with, but asked to keep part of its rump – which he took home and roasted. One of Tommy's other interests was Rugby League, and he headed a club in Workington. That Saturday, he went with the team for their match against Keighley. On the way he said he had a picnic for the team members. So they stopped and ate the food that Tommy provided – the lion sandwiches were quickly eaten!

Player Michael Smith had one of the shortest times ever playing for a professional Rugby League side. In early 1999 his two-year contract with Hull Sharks was ended after less than half an hour!

 When the Australian Rugby League team came to tour Britain in January 1968, they requested an extra piece of equipment – a fruit machine – which they installed in their hotel.

 President Nelson Mandela of South Africa wore a shirt with the number 6 at the Rugby Union World Cup final in 1995.

 At the mining area of Toowomba, Australia, the temperature is so hot that the Rugby League matches are played at 8 p.m. The late start can cause some mix-ups. At one game the Mount Isa team managed to have 17 men on the field.

Alex Melrose, the captain of RGS High Wycombe rugby side, was injured and out of a cup match in February 1999 – his toe had been broken by a cricket ball!

 The Cotton Traders leisurewear company was started by the former England prop Fran Cotton. He had to retire after he had a heart attack during a match in 1980.

 England lost a Rugby Union international for the first time at Twickenham in 1926. King George V was there to watch them lose to Scotland.

 The Great Britain women's Rugby League side had a good time in Australia in 1996, winning their series. The Great Britain men's side was not so happy. They had not won a series in Australia for 26 years – before most of the members of the women's side were born!

In 1889, during a match between the New Zealand Maoris and Yorkshire, the game was stopped as the referee went into the crowd to borrow a watch – his had broken!

 The Leeds Rugby League club owns the Headingley Test cricket ground.

 Angus Innes, the six foot six (1.98 metres) Australian captain of Cambridge University, was sent off in the Varsity match (the match against Oxford) in 1999. He was the first to be sent off in the match for over 100 years. The last was Justin Davies, sent off for fighting in 1894!

 The first try at Twickenham in an international to be scored direct from the kick-off was in the match between England and Wales in January 1910. England wing three-quarter P. B. Chapman scored.

Welsh Rugby League player John Westgarth, an impressive six foot five (1.95 metres) tall, is not to be tackled easily – he's a former pro boxer!

 In their second tour of Britain and France in 1924–5, the New Zealand All Blacks won all their 30 matches, with 721 points for and only 112 against.

 Rugby was included in the British sport stamps of 10 October 1980.

 Peter Rossborough, the Coventry full-back, was dropped by England. He had just scored 16 points in the match against France at Twickenham in February 1975.

The world schools rugby championships in 1998 included some unusually named teams, for example Glantaf, Colstons, Ratu, Prince Edward, Blackrock, Helpmekaar, Monument, Tupou and Highland (a United States school).

 A record 49,000 attended the amazing European rugby championships final in Dublin in January 1999. The Ulster team thrashed the French side Colombiers 21–6. The Ulster coach came all the way from Hollywood – Hollywood in County Down, that is!

 Willie John McBride scored his first try for Ireland when he played in his 62nd match for his country! It was in the Ireland vs. France match in March 1975. Ireland won 25–6.

Will Carling became the youngest ever national Rugby Union captain in 1988, when he became captain of England at 23.

Ninian Jamieson-Finlay played his first international Rugby Union match for Scotland against England when he was still at school – he was 17 years and 36 days old.

The fastest try ever scored was by Leicester no. 8 Leo Price in the match between England and Wales in 1923. After a kick-off into a strong wind, Leo chased the ball and attempted a drop goal. He missed, but ran on to catch the ball and score – all in under ten seconds.

The rugby team from Arnold School, Blackpool, didn't have a good time at a rugby tournament at Ipswich in 1995. Six of their players were taken to hospital – three with broken legs!

J. H. R. (Dick) Greenwood was dropped as England captain in 1969 – he had cut his eye playing squash! 'Budge' Rogers took over. Greenwood never played for England again.

 The women's rugby side in Worthing won a tourist award in the spring of 1998. It wasn't for their ability to play. A calendar showing them nude gave worldwide publicity to both the players and Worthing!

 The tallest man believed to have played in a rugby international was Richard Metcalfe who played for Scotland between 2000 and 2002. He was seven feet (2.13 metres) tall!

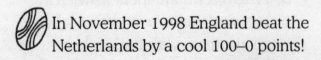 In November 1998 England beat the Netherlands by a cool 100–0 points!

Pierre Albadejo of France was the first player to kick three drop goals in one international, against Ireland at Paris in 1960.

 The Irish Rugby Union player Tony O'Reilly wrote an article for the programme for the Ireland vs. England match at Twickenham in 1970. Then he found himself playing in the game – for the first time in seven years!

 Britain issued a stamp to celebrate the centenary of the Rugby Football Union.

 Frank Sykes of Northampton had a long wait between internationals. He played in 1955 in the Scotland vs. France match and then, eight years later, for a totally different country – for New Zealand against Australia.

By 1986, John Morley, born in 1950, had scored 478 tries in senior rugby – including 378 for Bristol, a record for one club.

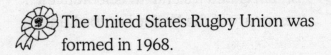 Bob Hiller of England scored in every one of his 19 internationals. This included 32 points in succession. He scored a total of 138 of the 199 points England managed over the 19 matches! When he retired in 1972, there was a headline: *Hiller 138 points, rest of England 61*.

The United States Rugby Union was formed in 1968.

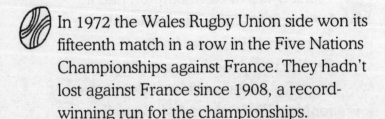 In 1972 the Wales Rugby Union side won its fifteenth match in a row in the Five Nations Championships against France. They hadn't lost against France since 1908, a record-winning run for the championships.

Neil Bennett scored 36 points for England in the match against Western Australia in May 1975.

 H. G. Periton was unique – the only Irishman to captain England in an international against Ireland!

 The first hat-trick of tries in the history of the Five Nations Championships was scored by Henry Taylor of England in 1881. It took a while for the second – scored by Chris Oti for England in the match against Ireland in 1988! It became known as the Six Nations in 2000 after Italy joined.

 After France lost all her international championships matches in 1957, a supporter ordered a two-metre wooden spoon, which held two litres, and presented it to the former French captain Jean Prat.

Rugby is said to have come from a game played by Roman soldiers in Britain, called 'Harpastum'. During the 1300s women joined in the game.

 Kevin Yates of Bath became well known in 1998. He was given a six-month ban for ear-biting.

 On 13 February 1931, the British Rugby Union clubs and national sides decided they could no longer play French clubs because they weren't good enough. A French team was not to play a British team again until 1946.

 Cyril Brownlie of New Zealand was the first international ever to be sent off, during a match against England at Twickenham. He was accused of hitting another player.

For the twelve Rugby Union tests the England team played in 1998, they used enough players for four different teams!

 The Scottish club Melrose began seven-a-side rugby at their ground, the Greenyards, in 1883. It was invented by player Edward Hay.

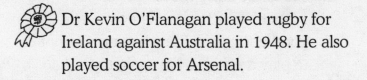

 Dr Kevin O'Flanagan played rugby for Ireland against Australia in 1948. He also played soccer for Arsenal.

 The US women's rugby champions thrashed a Scottish women's side 110–0 at Melrose in Scotland on 11 April 1994.

In 1968 at Dublin the referee
Mike Titcomb allowed a drop
goal by Gareth Edwards in the
Wales vs. Ireland match. This was
a surprise, since even the Welsh
players thought Edwards had
missed the kick!

 Henry Vassall, the Oxford and England
player, first thought up the idea of passing
the ball in the early 1880s.

 Two of the most famous of the Welsh
fly halves, Carwyn James and Barry
John, both came from the same
village – Cefniethin.

Rugby Union dates:

1870 Rugby Union introduced to New Zealand by John Munro, who learned the game at Sherborne School, England.

1893 Referees were allowed to make their own decisions, without the help of umpires.

1897 Team numbers introduced to rugby when Queensland, Australia, played New Zealand at Brisbane.

1900 Rugby Union first played at the Olympics.

1909 The first ever game at Twickenham – between Richmond and Harlequins.

1921 Numbered shirts first used in an international – England vs. Wales at Cardiff.

 The New Zealand All Blacks were up to something different in 1998 – they launched a range of perfumes and deodorants for men. The perfumes were known as 'the great smell of brutes'!

By all accounts the first people to play rugby in Fiji were the police.

 When rugby began, teams were of 20 a side, and there were three fullbacks allowed!

 On 4 January 1998, all rugby matches in Britain appeared to be a washout, with wet weather and floods. Only one match was played that day, between Neath and Llanelli in Wales. They managed to get round the weather problem by playing in a sandpit – there were three tons of sand on the pitch!

 In 1932, the heads of Rugby Union in Britain banned the use of floodlights – yet the first rugby match played using floodlights had taken place as early as 1878!

In 1893, Billy Haus, who played for Penryn RFC, Cornwall, won a competition for the longest kick in British rugby – he managed 79 yards and 30 inches (73 metres).

 The club motto of the Barbarians is: 'Rugby football is a game for gentlemen in all classes, but never for a bad sportsman in any class.'

 The Reverend Canon George Ogilvie introduced a game which mixed up rugby and soccer in South Africa in 1861. It was known as 'Gog's Game'.

 James and Stewart Boyce are the only twin brothers to appear together in a Rugby Union international, for Australia against New Zealand in 1964.

There are 13 players in a Rugby League side and 15 in Rugby Union.

The Calcutta Cup trophy is awarded to the winner of the annual Scotland vs. England Rugby Union match. It is made from melted-down silver Indian rupees.

 Probably the most expensive rugby match took place on 15 July 1997 when a college match in Tonga turned into a riot and the college was burned down by supporters. The cost of the destruction was put at about £480,000.

Peter Squires, who played Rugby Union for England as wing, also played cricket for Yorkshire.

Keith Savage of Northamptonshire scored a try during a Friday night match for London Irish. He was in line for a rest, but was called up the next day to play for England against Wales.

 Johnny Wilkinson, Newcastle's young kicking star, missed a penalty kick for the first time at Twickenham in May 1999 against Wasps. The miss allowed Wasps to win the Tetley Bitter Cup.

 In the England vs. Wales match at Twickenham in 1970, the French referee Robert Calmet retired injured! Referee R. F. 'Johnny' Johnson took his place.

Rugby League dates:

1896   Rugby League Challenge Cup launched.

1906   Rugby League teams reduced from 15 to 13 a side.

1922   The name Rugby League football is adopted.

1964   Substitutes allowed in Rugby League.

1967   K. Jarrett, a Welsh Rugby Union player, signs to Barrow Rugby League side.

1968   Colin Dixon signs a record Rugby League transfer from Halifax to Salford for £15,000.

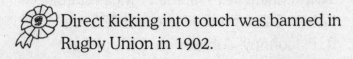 Six players from the Gala club played for Scotland against England in two matches in 1971.

Direct kicking into touch was banned in Rugby Union in 1902.

London Scottish Player Mick Watson managed to be sent off in record time in a match against Bath in 1999 – after only 42 seconds!

Ten players from Cardiff played in the Welsh XV against Scotland at Murrayfield in 1948.

A record 104,053 spectators attended the Scotland vs. Wales Rugby Union match at Murrayfield on 1 March 1975. Scotland won 12–0. This is still the largest ever crowd to attend Murrayfield.

The first England vs. Ireland international was played in 1875 at a cricket ground – the Oval, London.

Leeds won the Rugby League Challenge Cup in 1999 with a record 52–16 win over London Broncos. They managed to beat or equal five records in their win. Iestyn Harris kicked a record eight goals and his twenty points equalled the individual record in the cup. Broncos had one excuse – their skipper Shaun Edwards played the match with a broken thumb.

 In the early 1950s, almost four million people watched Rugby League games in Britain.

 The oval-shaped rugby ball, with its pig's bladder interior, was considered unusual enough to be shown at the International Exhibition in London in 1851.

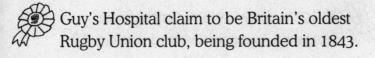

The first rugby matches had two umpires with sticks. They decided if a referee had made a right decision. The umpires then became touch judges and their sticks had flags attached to them.

The ground is now known for athletics, but the first England rugby match against the All Blacks took place at Crystal Palace, London, in 1905.

Guy's Hospital claim to be Britain's oldest Rugby Union club, being founded in 1843.

Western Samoa set a rugby record on 7 July 1993. They beat a team in Marborough, New Zealand, 128–0, breaking the record set by the All Blacks in a game against Western New South Wales, Australia, in 1962 of 125–0.

Early rugby matches at Rugby School could involve 300 players! There were no positions.

 The All Blacks begin international or major matches with a 'haka' – a Maori war dance. The first line of the haka is: 'Ringa pakia waewae takahia!'

 In 1973 all five nations in the Five Nations Championships were tied. All five sides won their home matches.

 Hacking was banned in rugby after Richmond club reported one player being killed and 20 others injured as a result of kicking or tripping up an opponent!

Tony O'Reilly had the longest career of any Irish Rugby Union international – lasting from 1955 to 1970. On the day he first appeared in an international, against France, another Irish team member was W. O'Connell. O'Connell played only 55 minutes before he was injured. He never played rugby for Ireland again. His was the shortest international appearance for Ireland!

Shaun Edwards of Wigan appeared in 29 successive Rugby League finals in the ten years from 1985 to 1994.

Harry Read, who played 13 times for the Irish rugby side from 1910 to 1913, also played cricket and tennis for Ireland.

The first England vs. Scotland match at Edinburgh had 20 a side.

Rugby was first played regularly in Japan in 1924.

 In February 1999 the players in a Rugby League match between Doncaster Dragons and Oldham St Anne's were dragged from their showers to continue their match – which was level at 15–15 after 80 minutes and went to extra time. The referee had decided they should play on for a result.

 Rugby players Jack Gregory of England and Ken Jones of Ireland both won silver medals at the 1948 Olympics, as part of the 4 x 100 metre relay squad.

 Red and yellow cards were introduced to the Rugby Union Courage League matches in Britain on 7 January 1995.

During the 1860s rugby teams could have 25 or more players.

 The Australian Rugby League side is known as the Kangaroos.

 English rugby player Jason Leonard holds the English record for most caps – 114.

 In early 1994 Alex Murphy, a British Rugby League commentator and pundit, claimed that the Australian TV audience for the deciding Great Britain vs. Australia international was between 20 and 30 million. There was something very odd about this claim – the population of the whole of Australia at the time was only 17,661,000!

The first player to play fifty times for his country was Tom Kiernan for Ireland in the Ireland vs. England match at Twickenham on 12 February 1972.

 Peter Heindorff was born in Germany. He came to England when young and was the captain of Bath Rugby Union side in the early 1970s.

 Alec Lewis made his first appearance for England aged 31 in 1952. He was lucky to be there at all – he'd been injured by a landmine in World War II.

 Wasps rugby club run their own fleet of taxis in and around London – decorated with the Wasps logo and black and yellow colours.

Peter Dixon played only one match for the British Lions in Australia in 1975. He flew 24,000 miles for the last match of the tour, against a Queensland County XV.

 A player called M. A. English actually played for Ireland. K. J. F. Scotland, though, played for Scotland!

 The All Blacks had their worst losing streak since 1949 in August 1998 – by losing all of three games in a row, two to Australia and one to South Africa!

 Brian Bevan holds the record for Rugby League tries – a massive 796.

 C. Charlie Faulkner was probably the most difficult man to challenge when he played for Wales. He was also a judo black belt!

Teams of 15 a side for Rugby Union were introduced for the Oxford vs. Cambridge match in 1875.

 Graham Dawe, the Bath hooker, became the first English international to be shown a yellow card – in the England vs. Scotland match on 8 January 1995. A month later John Davies of Wales became the first to receive a red card in the Five Nations Championships.

 The Oxford vs. Cambridge 'Varsity' match was first played in 1872.

 In early 1995 Sheffield Hallam rugby players won their appeal for their game to be rescheduled – they were too drunk to play the first time!

In 1974 the British Lions in South Africa had a code: 99. If it was called all the pack were to attack the opposition! It was thought if they all fought together, they'd never all be sent off!

 Junior Rugby Union player are known as colts.

 The Soviet rugby team for the first women's world cup, held in Wales, were given free meals at restaurants because they were so short of money.

 Runcorn, the Rugby League side, failed to win a match for two and a half years. They finally beat Dewsbury 9–2 on 3 March 1991.

In the 1990s, with the formation of the
Super League for Rugby League and
professional Rugby Union, the animal
kingdom invaded the names of teams. The
new names included:

1. Warrington Wolves
2. Lancashire Lynx
3. York Wasps
4. Swinton Lions
5. Keighley Cougars
6. Batley Bulldogs
7. Hunslet Hawks
8. Northern Bulls

Others names included Salford Reds,
Barrow Braves and Whitehaven Warriors.

 David Watkins, of Newport and Wales,
was the first to play in the British Lions at
both Rugby Union and Rugby League –
in 1965 and 1966.

In 1974, by mistake, John C. Bevan was called up for the Rugby Union British Lions tour of South Africa. He was then playing Rugby League for Warrington. The person supposed to be picked was John D. Bevan of Wales.

 The Five Nations Championships became the four nations championships in 1931 after France was banned for a year for foul play. The French didn't return to the Five Nations until 1947. It then became the Six Nations in 2000 after Italy joined.

 Canadian Neil Jenkins scored a world record of 8 penalty goals in the 26–24 defeat of Wales at Cardiff on 10 November 1993.

 Referee Peter Richmond sent off all 30 players in a match between Abingdon and Didcot – they were suspended for 30 days.

Rugby is said to have started in 1823 when William Webb Ellis, a 17-year-old pupil at Rugby School, picked up the ball while playing football. He did so because he knew the game would soon end and he wanted his side to win. A plaque was put up to commemorate his achievement. Rugby was well known for the unusual – in 1797 a battalion of English soldiers with fixed bayonets were called to the school to put down a riot by pupils!

 The All Blacks once beat South Australia 117–6.

 Dave Travis played for Richmond Rugby Union team. In the 1970s he also threw the javelin, and represented Britain at the Olympics.

The England rugby captain of the 1980s, Bill Beaumont, was once described as 'John Wayne, Goliath and Sampson rolled into one'. He was also said to have the biggest bottom in rugby!

 China became the 76th official rugby-playing nation in March 1997.

 Gareth Edwards, the great Wales and British Lions rugby star of the 1970s, always preferred fishing to rugby.

 Hussein M. Barhi set a record 74 points for Fulham against the London Broncos Rugby League side in 1981.

Alan Old played as fly-half for the England rugby side against Scotland at Murrayfield in 1974. That same day, his brother Chris was in the England cricket side playing against the West Indies. Alan also played cricket for Durham, in the summer.

 Some rugby players have very large feet – Hudson Smith, the Australian star with the Salford Reds, wears size 14 boots.

 In the early days of Rugby Union, the only score was called a goal. Touching down the ball behind the opposition line gave the kicker a 'try' at the goalposts. This was where the word try came from.

 Oriel club managed to play for 800 minutes in matches between 1971 and 1973 without giving away a try.

Henry Garnett of Bradford was selected for Scotland in 1877. He played most of his international games in bare feet!

 The United States women's rugby team is known as the Eagles.

 Patrick Sebastien, president of the French rugby club Brive, isn't shy. In February 1999 he married his girlfriend Natalie on the pitch in front of 18,000 spectators!

William Tyrrell played for Ireland against Wales in 1914. The game was described as 'the roughest match ever'. It didn't seem to harm Tyrrell. He went on to become an Air Vice-Marshal in the RAF and was given a knighthood.

William Cerutti, prop for Australia 17 times, was absolutely, definitely not superstitious. He always insisted on wearing the no. 13 jersey!

 The soccer international between Scotland and Wales on 27 May 1997 took place at Rugby Park!

 Trevor Rees-Jones, the only survivor of the car crash which killed Princess Diana in Paris in 1997, was the captain of the Oswestry rugby team.

 Every September a team of players from all sorts of places, called Captain Crawshay's Welsh XV, tour the West Country of England.

From the 552 matches in the Argentine rugby championships of 1980, 251 players managed to be sent off!

Ken Chapman, who looked after the Rugby Football Union in 1974–5, was the son of the former Arsenal soccer manager Herbert Chapman.

 The old London Wasps ground in London was called Sudbury; London Irish's ground in London is called Sunbury. The grounds are 15 minutes apart.

 Leeds Rhinos, the Rugby League club, signed Pestyn Harris for a record £325,000 on 3 April 1997.

 Among the oddest rugby supporters of all time was the Reverend Frederick Westcoot, the headmaster of Sherborne School in Somerset. He supported the team wearing a cycling outfit and a rat catcher's hat.

The first Rugby League international was played in April 1904, when England played Other Nationalities at Wigan. The crowd was 12,000. England lost 9–3.

 The Rugby Union season in Britain always begins on September 1st or 2nd.

 The Golden Wasps trophy is awarded for the winner of the Wasps vs. Newport match.

 Gerry Brand, the 1931–2 South African full-back, kicked the ball 90 yards to score at Twickenham. It is believed to be the longest ever dropped goal.

 The England Rugby Union team lost for the first time since 1991 in February 1997, when they were beaten 17–15 by France at Northampton.

The first Rugby Union county match
to be played under floodlights was
Cumberland & Westmoreland
vs. Lancashire at Workington in
November 1959.

 Sam Doble of Moseley scored a reputed
3,651 tries in his Rugby Union career. He
retired after injury in 1976.

 Frans Ten Bos, a Dutchman, played
Rugby Union for Scotland 17 times. He
was eligible because he had lived in
Scotland and also served in the Argyll
Scottish regiment in the British Army.

In 1970 Semesk Sikivou of the Fijians hit the bar with the ball while taking a penalty kick in a match against the Combined Services at Portsmouth. The bar fell down! Play was suspended. The bar was mended. The kick was retaken and was kicked over. The Fijians won 11–6.

 When he came out of retirement for the 1973–4 season for Llanelli, Delme Thomas scored seven tries – it was more than he'd scored in his previous twelve years with the club!

Will Carling was England Rugby Union captain for a record 59 times. He was captain when England became the first team to win back-to-back grand slams in 1992.

Dick Uzzell skipped a day from St Luke's College, Exeter, to play Rugby Union for Newport on 3 October 1963. His drop goal in the match resulted in the only All Blacks defeat of their tour of Great Britain!

 The first £1,000 transfer in Rugby League was for Harold Buck, who moved as winger for Hunslett to Leeds.

 Keith Hatter of the Moseley club scored over a thousand points in the 1970–71 season!

 The man who headed the Scottish Rugby Football Union in 1975–6 was also chief constable for the area that included the Scotland ground, Murrayfield.

Bob Hiller, playing for Harlequins, managed to miss eleven goal kicks in the match against Gloucester in October 1969. He stayed on to practise kicking afterwards. He must have been worth watching, as a lot of the crowd stayed to see him practise.

 Nigel Horton of England became the first man to be sent off at Twickenham for 47 years in 1974. The last had been Cyril Brownlie of New York in 1925!

 Rodney Webb, playing for the West Midlands in January 1967, found he was up against an Australian side which included his brother Richard.

When the Barbarians played Penarth in Wales in April 1982, they were leading 84–16 when the Barbarians captain David Johnston asked the referee to end the game five minutes early to spare Penarth further embarrassment.

 Brothers Colin and Stan Meads both played for the All Blacks. Between them they played 70 times for their country.

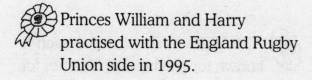 Princes William and Harry practised with the England Rugby Union side in 1995.

 The first Rugby Union match between England and France took place in 1906.

Because of the huge crowds for the sport, the Rugby League Challenge Cup finals were moved to Wembley in 1929. In the first London final Wigan beat Dewsbury 13–2.

 In 22 days David Ainge of Bristol reached 100 points for his club. He managed this feat by 24 September 1968.

 The first Rugby League game played in France took place on 31 December 1933 in Paris, between England and Australia! England were thrashed 63–13.

 Alan Williams should have been known for playing 800 matches for his club and 50 for his country. But he made headlines when he became the referee who sent off four Falmouth and three Bideford players during their match at Falmouth in October 1975.

Rugby is reckoned to be the fourth most dangerous sport for neck injuries.

 The Argentine touring team is known as the Pumas.

 Playing against England in the 1932 Rugby League tour, Queensland forward Dan Dempsey broke his arm. Going off the pitch, he had it set. He then insisted on going back on the field. Tearing off the bandages and throwing away his splint he said, 'At least I can get in someone's way.' In the same match Australian Eric Weissel played with a broken ankle and the lock forward Frank O'Connor refused to remain on the stretcher as he was carried off the field.

 After over 100 years, until 1998, Leicester and Bristol rugby clubs remained the only teams in Britain to use letters instead of numbers on the players' shirts.

One of the great stars of English rugby in the 1930s was Prince Alexander Obolensky. He had been born in Russia and never officially became English. He was killed at the age of only 24 in an air accident in March 1940 when flying for the RAF.

The first French Rugby Union tour of English was in March 1934 – they won one of their six games.

After the French internationals Paties and Sutra were suspended in 1975 for menacing and insulting the referee at Narbonne, France, they were told they could only play again if they passed exams and refereed themselves for a while!

Some players' nicknames:
Bonzo – C. R. Johns, Cornwall club player
The Rock – Alfred Roques, France
   international
The Boot – Olley Geffin, South African
   international
The Two Fleas – Guy and Lilian Camberabo,
   French brothers and internationals
Monsieur Drop – Pierre Albaladejo, French
   international
Wigs – W. A. Mulcahy, Ireland international

 The Rugby League player Jim
Valentine was nicknamed 'The Lion of
Swinton'.

 Darren Clarke, who won a 400 metres
gold medal at the Commonwealth Games
at Auckland in 1990, joined Balmain, the
Australian Rugby League side in 1991. In
his first match he scored a try after only
two minutes!

Before the evacuation of Dunkirk in 1940, a British military rugby team beat a French military rugby team in Paris 36–3. It was the first match between a British and French side in nine years.

 Some names of grounds:
Helfire Corner – Redruth, Cornwall
Webb Ellis Road – Rugby
Jock's Lodge – Royal High club, Edinburgh
The Brewery Field – Bridgend, Wales
Donnybrook – Bective Rangers club, Dublin, Eire

 Eddie Waring became well known as a Rugby League commentator for the BBC from the 1960s to the 1980s. In 1943 he managed the Dewsbury Rugby League club.

The All Blacks began their shortest tour of Britain on 29 August 1939. They played and won only two matches before war broke out on 2 September, and they left England on 13 September.

 An England Rugby Union side played South Africa during World War II. It was a little unusual – the match took place on board the ship the *New Amsterdam*.

 The nickname for the Twickenham Rugby Union ground is 'Billy Williams' cabbage patch'.